WORDS CAN NOT DEFINE HER....

AN ANTHOLOGY OF POEMS

EDITED AND COMPILED BY :
DR. SONIA GUPTA

DEDICATED TO

Every Woman of The World

Contents

Contents

Contents

Foreword

"Words Cannot Define Her : A Specific Anthology"

"A woman is the full circle.
Within her is the ability to create, nurture and transform."
(Diane Mariechild)

The importance of women in the universe can be well understood in the context of the above statement. The Manusmriti, an important book in the Indian tradition, states that "Yatra naryastu pujyante ramante tatra Devata, yatraitaastu na pujyante sarvaastatrafalaah kriyaah", which means where women are honored, Gods reside there, and where women are dishonored, all actions fail. Presently, discussion on women is an important issue under social discussion. When we sit down to have a meaningful conversation on an issue, first of all there are questions related to its importance and relevance. In between these two questions, a question is related to social inequality. The prevailing social inequality between men and women is not from the beginning of creation, but it is the result of different stages of social development. Ironically, the society became dynamic in the stage of social development, but the patriarchal society limited the rights of women; The result of which was that in terms of importance and authority, the social status of women kept falling day by day. Even in this zenith of development of the twenty-first century, the status of women probably still has not been as high as the Rigvedic society. After the post-Vedic period, in the Sutra period and after that in the middle ages, the continuous decline in the status of women has not been compensated till date.

In this long span of time, the life of a woman has gone through many ups and downs. Current circumstances are different. In the 21st century, changes have taken place very rapidly all over the world. There has been a change in the attitude towards women. It's a century of self-respect and confidence with challenges. In the midst of all these things, the responsibilities increase. American business executive, billionaire, and philanthropist Sheryl Kara Sandberg says very right:- "We need women at all levels, including the top, to change the dynamic, reshape the conversation, to make sure women's voices are heard and heeded, not overlooked and ignored." In an era of eroding values, it's very important to have trust in mutual relations between men and women. Every path of progress depends on the understanding of both. The noise of freedom often drowns out the real issues. We should take it seriously and positively. Women have given direction to the society in every era. They give speed to the world. Jeff Gaines writes with great sincerity:-

"You taught us to tie our shoes and look after our sisters and brothers.
And that unless we are standing for something correct, we must always
be kind to others."

Literature has always emphasized the importance of existence of women. It has a long tradition in literature. Poetess Dr. Sonia Gupta's plan to bring out an anthology of various poets on these issues will definitely take this process further. She has done a special job by bringing together various poets from India and abroad in a compilation on one subject. The poems in the anthology make one feel that as an editor she understood her responsibility very well and used her capabilities to the fullest. Previously she has also proved herself as a writer & poet through various publications. Through anthology "Words Cannot Define Her", various aspects of women, their existence and importance, contemporary problems and their solutions have been discussed. A woman lives many characters in herself and proves her worth in all characters. The poets of the compilation have represented the various dimensions of female world with their full potential.

I am sure the anthology will be widely read and appreciated. Hearty congratulations and endless wishes to Dr. Sonia Gupta for editing a wonderful anthology and to all the eminent poets included in it.

- Dr. Shailesh Gupta Veer.
(Poet, Reviewer & Editor)

Preface

❧❧❧

"There's something special about a woman who dominates in a man's world.
It takes a certain grace, strength, intelligence, fearlessness, and the nerve to
never take no for an answer."

(Rihanna)

❧❧❧

Very well said by the famous musical artist 'Rihanna' through the above quote
that a WOMAN's existence can't be underestimated. Definitely, she harbours
such virtues which make her special in being dominated even in a man's
world.

The word 'WOMAN' seems to be ordinary, but it has a unique meaning.
The WOMAN is God's angel sent by him into this mythical world who is
blessed with a number of virtues. Even in a WO-MAN, 'MAN' exists. She
is a WOMAN only, who gives birth to a MAN. It is often said that this
world is MAN-predominated. But in the true sense, this world is all owing to
WOMAN.

Since her birth, she blossoms in many relations playing vivid roles like a
daughter, mother, sister and partner. As a daughter, being the angel of her
parents, she fills their life with joy, love and a smile. As a sister, she threads a
garland of love and care. As a partner, she accompanies her soulmate in every
odd and even phase of life and enlightens a candle of love in his world. As

a mother, she is an embodiment of blessings, love and care for her children. In nutshell, it can be beautifully said that in every form, she is a paragon of LOVE.

Alas! despite knowing her strengths and virtues, this world always underestimates her and tries to suppress her identity. Many times, she becomes the victim of this society's crimes and injustice toward her. Her heart and soul get pierced with those unhealed wounds. Yet igniting her inner power, she fights against all the odds and wins every war. History reveals, how she has shown her power in the form of 'DURGA', 'LAKSHMI BAI', 'SATI', and many more. Her inner strength can't be defined in a few words only.

Today, the time has changed drastically and the WOMAN of today is not considered to be docile and caged in four walls. She is touching the heights of success, wearing the wings of self-belief and determination. She is like the previous Prime Ministar of India, thr late 'Indira Gandhi' and 'the present President 'Droupadi Murmu' who have shown their potential of leading this Man-predominated world through their WOMAN power. There are several such names all around. In conclusion, if we try to define a WOMAN in the words, it is impossible to do so. Because she is not only a WOMAN but a paragon of abundant virtues.

I have got fifteen independent poetry books, several anthologies, and other literary contributions on vivid themes. But for a long time, this was one of my dreams as a WOMAN poet to gather an anthology of poems on WOMAN composed by different pens. That inspired me to take an initiative for compiling and editing this anthology. The current anthology "Words Cannot Define Her", is a collection of 50 poems dedicated to WOMEN. These poems have been composed by 50 poets from different countries of the world. The versatile poets have dipped their emotions into the ink of their pen, and have painted such a wonderful canvas, that represents the beauty and value of this small word that is known as 'WOMAN'. This is not only a book but a tribute and honour to all the WOMEN of the world.

I hope, after reading these beautiful verses composed by beautiful souls, your heart will enchant the songs of WOMAN saluting her for all the virtues she has been gifted by the great Almighty. And I believe, that through these verses, the vision of society towards WOMEN will definitely change to a positive side.

Yours sincerely
Dr. Sonia Gupta

Acknowledgements

Gratitude is a single word, but deep meaning it beholds. I usually hear these words – "If we say Thank you to someone, it means we are bowing our head in front of that Lord only". We can forget anything in life, but we should never forget to thank someone who has helped or motivated us in any way.

I am a medical professional, I never thought that one day I would become a writer, poet and author. It is all a miracle and a dream for me. But now it has become my passion, inspiration and an integral part of my life. It's all by God's grace that he honoured me with such a unique gift.

First of all, I thank the Goddess of knowledge and wisdom *Maa Saraswati,*who gave me the strength to complete this work and encouraged me to pick up my pen to compile, edit, and prepare this anthology.

In the world, everything changes, but one thing that never ever changes is *our parents.* Heartfelt thanks to my parents for their faith and showering their infinite blessings on me. Special thanks to my father who has left this materialistic world attaining the embrace of the divine Lord. He had been my inspiration and will be forever and his teachings illuminate my life's pathway like an enlightening candle. My mother is my best friend, who has always accompanied me in every odd and even phase of life. At every step of this project, her guidance and blessings were with me. She motivated me to complete this huge task. I am blessed to have my two younger brothers who are pillars of my life. They are younger than me, but the biggest booster of inspiration, who encouraged me to accomplish even the impossible tasks in my life. A token of thanks to my dear brothers.

Huge bundle of gratitude to all the authors and poets, who have put their endless efforts by contributing their wonderful poems signifying the theme of this anthology. Most of the poets are much senior to me and I pay my regard and honour to all of them for their full cooperation from the day one of this project till the last moment, respecting my guidelines and instructions. Each poem is filled with vivid colours of emotions, respect, love, appreciation and honour toward femineity which has painted a beautiful canvas that would be worthwhile to preserve forever in the hearts of readers. Without all of you, this collection would not have been possible. Once again, my heartfelt thanks to all of you for your love support, and encouragement.

My words are not enough to thank *Dr. Shailesh Veer Gupta* sir, for writing a wonderful foreword for this anthology. Without his support and blessings, this anthology was not possible. He not only reviewed these poems but also guided me at every step in completing this project. He is not only a good writer but a humble personality who always encourages other writers. A heartful thanks to you dear sir.

Teachers are the selfless builders of our life, A word of thanks to all respected teachers who always showed me the right path in my life and brimmed my heart with their blessings.

Friends are the precious ornaments gifted by God, who without any blood relation, make a bonding of forever relation. My regards and love to all friends far and near.

Last but not least, it will be unfair if I forget to thank the *Notion Press publication* through which this book is going to be published. Thanks to entire team for the cooperation.

Thank you, readers, fellow poets, and friends for all your love and appreciation!!!

Dr. Sonia Gupta

Know About The Editor

Dr. Sonia Gupta (Mohali, Punjab, India)

Dr. Sonia Gupta is a writer, poetess, reviewer, editor and translator. She writes in English, Hindi, and Punjabi languages. By profession she is a Dentist (MDS) with major specialization in Oral and Maxillofacial Pathology. Poetry is her passion. She has established herself as a renowned author after getting her fifteen independent books published, out of which five are in Hindi and ten are in English language. Her English books are poetic collections entitled 'Spectrum of Life', 'Canvas of Life..With My Pen', 'Fountain of Inspirations', 'Meeting My Soulmate', 'Silent Verses', 'Mysterious Musings of Life', 'Agony of Life', 'Miracle of Virtues', 'Acrostic Motivations', and 'There is No Darkness'. Her Hindi books include four collections of poetry entitled 'Zindagi Gulzar Hai', 'Ummid Ka Diya', 'Kabhi Jalte Kabhi Bujhte Chirag' and 'Kuch Ankahe Ehsas'. One of her books of stories 'Aadmi Bne Rehne Ka Dhong' has been published recently.

Her literary journey continues with a great endeavour. For her, poetry is a God-gifted boon and she wishes to fly high wearing the wings of poetry. She writes in vivid genera of literature like poetry, stories, essays, letters, songs and many more. Her writings reflect her closeness and deep love for nature, life, spirituality and humanity. She is an active member of various poetry groups on Facebook and has won several awards in writing competitions organized by those groups and other literary platforms. She won a Gold and Silver Medal in a Poetic world Cup contest held by Nigeria in Feb and May 2018 respectively, PRASANNA JENN MEMORIAL AWARD -2018 by the Asian Literary Society, and 5th rank in the International Essay writing competition on 'Skin complexion discrimination' organized by literary society, India in March 2018. One of her essays 'Our role & responsibilities toward nation was selected in a National essay writing competition and is a part of the book 'Youth as Nation Builders; a collection of 41 essays published by Lab Academia.

She has contributed to more than 100 National and International anthologies so far. She is a regular contributor to monthly online magazines like 'Hall of Poets', 'Reflection' and 'Glomag' and International Journals like 'Research Inspiration', 'Research Imbibition' and 'Jai Maa Saraswati Gyandayani'. Her writings have been published in various National and International newspapers. She has translated many poems of other poets from different regions of world into English, Hindi and Punjabi languages. Many other projects are underway.

Besides poetry, she is fond of painting, singing, cooking, knitting, designing, stitching and embroidery. She has won many awards in Art competitions. Many of her paintings have been placed on the cover pages of various anthologies. Even she has designed the cover page of her two English anthologies entitled "Fountain of Inspirations" and "Canvas of Life..With My Pen". She is actively contributing to the literature via her literary YouTube channel, Facebook page, Blog and Instagram profile.

Dr. Sonia has gone through many ups and downs in her life that directed her vision toward suffering and she expresses that with her pen. She considers her parents her biggest inspiration, who have always motivated her in each and every phase of her life. She lost her father in 2019, who was an English professor. She is living her life following his teachings and footprints. She has got two younger brothers, but for her, they are the pillars of her life.

Dr. Sonia Gupta is a renowned name in her professional field also. She is working as an Associate Professor in the Oral Pathology Dept. at a Dental College in Mohali. She serves the community as a doctor by providing dental care. She has 22 scientific publications in PubMed and Scopus indexed National and International Journals with the first authorship and many more are under review. She is also working on three textbooks on her subject of specialization. She is acting as a reviewer of various Medical and Dental Journals. She actively takes part in various conferences, workshops, community health programs, and events and has presented several research papers and posters. She is a dedicated academician with a mission of making her students excel in their subjects and in developing their multitalented skills.

CONTACT DETAILS

- **ADDRESS**- #95/3, Adarsh Nagar, Dera Bassi, Dist: Mohali, Punjab-140507, India.
- **MOBILE-** 6280420736
- **FACEBOOK ID** - 100004964983747@facebook.com
- **FACEBOOK PAGE** - https://www.facebook.com/sonia4840/
- **BLOG** - http://drsoniablogspot.blogspot.in/
- **E MAIL** - drsoniagupta82@gmail.com
- **YOUTUBE CHANNEL**https://www.youtube.com/channel/ UCKF2jM5P8VDjZ9fBZLBTRHA
- **INSTAGRAM ID-**https://instagram.com/ gdrsonia?igshid=YmMyMTA2M2Y=

Words Cannot Define Her

O' she is the special creation of God,
Without whom is incomplete this entire world,
She has the power of giving birth even to a MAN,
She is proudly known to be a WOMAN.

As a daughter, sister, partner and mother.
She blossoms vivid relationships like a blooming flower,
An embodiment of sacrifices, love and care,
She never leaves any life to be bare.

Hiding her own tears, she brings smiles to everyone,
She turns a house into divine heaven,
An enlightening candle in the gloom of dark,
Mesmerizes hearts with her magnificent spark.

She is soft-hearted as tender petals,
But by igniting her inner strength she can bring miracles,
O' words cannot define her fully,
She has been blessed with virtues abundantly.

© **Dr. Sonia Gupta**

An Intro About The Reviewer

Dr. Shailesh Gupta Veer (Fatehpur, UP, India)

❧❧❧

He is a poet, critic and multi-prize winner. He has a PhD in Archaeology. His literary works are characterized with a high degree of creativity and aunthencity. He is a bilingual, writes in English & Hindi both. He is a blogger, where he regulars posts his poems. He is Admin and Moderator of various poetry groups on Facebook. He has edited about two dozen literary books and several magazines time to time. His poetry has been published in various literary magazines, journals, anthologies and websites. He has won many awards in the field of poetry and literature. His poems have been translated into Chinese, Greek, German, French, Azerbaijani, Arabic, Italian, Serbian, Croatian, Portuguese, Nepali, Punjabi & some other languages. He is the editor of Micro poetry Cosmos and the associate editor of The Voice of Creative Research. He is also a reviewer and promoter of poetry and literature. His poetry attracts hearts of many, while forcing brains to get calculative. His love for human values, nature, philosophy and the spiritual world is insurmountable. All these can clearly be seen in his works of poetry. He was declared a Literary Icon in December 2018 by TV program You and Literature Today from Nigeria. His poems were read on The Dear John Show of Warrington, England. He is an inspiration for the budding writers.

CONTACT DETAILS

- **Address:** 18/17, Radha Nagar, Fatehpur (UP) Pin Code- 212601
- **Mobile:** 9839942005
- **Email:** editorsgveer@gmail.com

You Are Complete Poetry

I am word

You are dictionary

I am sound

You are meaning

I am blank paper

You are pen

I am keypad

You are fingers

I am simple sentence

You're rhythm & rhymes

I am grammar

You are literature

You spread the words in the air

I capture them

I think only

You are power of thought

I am poetic scenes only

You are complete poetry

Without you I am nothing.

© Dr. Shailesh Gupta Veer

List Of Poets

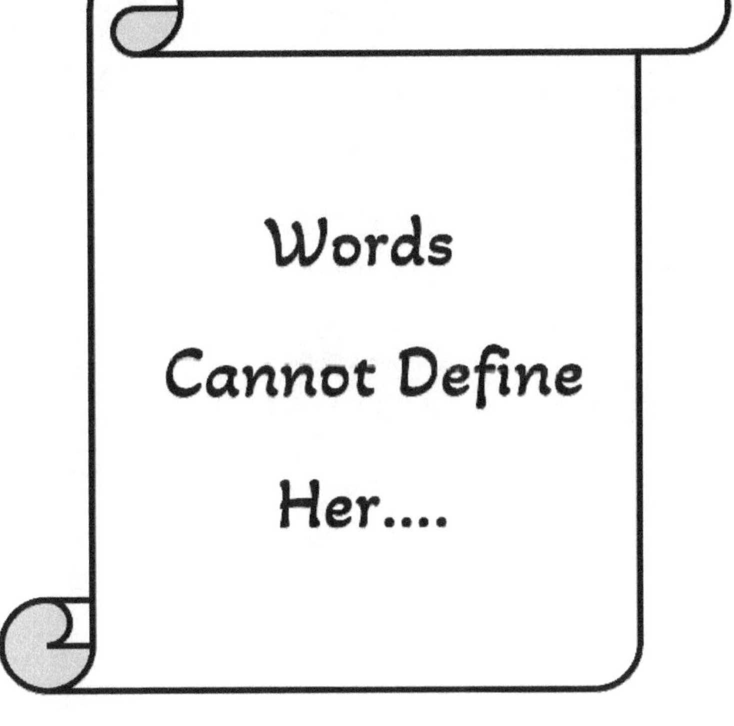
Words
Cannot Define
Her.....

1. Beautiful In and Out

I am a woman! Men in awe of my beauty,
Even the creatures dance to the rhythm of my melody,
Calmly, lovely and pretty,
I come with the remedy.

I am a woman, with a heart of gold,
Beautiful in and out, charming beauty untold,
God's specially and wonderfully made creation,
Perfected and endowed, worthy of emulation.

I am a woman!
Beautiful and wonderful,
My appearance: arresting and appealing,
My adherence: assuring and enduring.

A lovely Queen reserved for the King,
A priceless Princess preserved for a Prince,
In the palace, I will flaunt my royalty,
In brilliance, I will express my loyalty.

©Ajayi Oluwasegun Samson

Ajayi Oluwasegun Samson (Osogtbo, Osun, Nigeria)

ajayiolusegun49@gmail.com

He is a poet and a creative writer. Poetry is his passion. He writes poems, essays and stories since secondary school. He has won several prizes and awards during his schooling both at the National and Local levels, in debate competitions and essay writing. He is an active member of several poetry groups on Facebook. Presently, he is pursuing Nursing.

2. A Hundred Dreams

A hundred dreams, poised and dainty,
I wove carefully,
Not a stitch, out of place.
Not a colour mismatched,
Not a thread hung loose.

I wove my dreams with a beauteous vision,
And compelling dreams,
When I spread my knitted wings.

A storm came snapping by.
The maddening race overtook me,
And scattered my tapestry,
hither and thither.

The patterns I held,
clutched to my heart,
Scattered into smithereens,
Lost forever.

© Dr. Balesh Jindal

Dr. Balesh Jindal (Delhi, India)

jindalbalesh@yahoo.co.in

She is a renowned artist with a creative portfolio of art, poetry and photographs. She has published three poetry books; a coffee table book 'A Hundred Dreams', 'Dear Father' and 'The Reluctant Doctor a Memoir'. She is a physician by profession; a graduate of the prestigious Lady Hardinge Medical College in Delhi and has had a professional medical practice for the last forty years. She has received several awards in her professional and literary fields.

3. To the Loving Husband

Let there be no valuables! what of that?
Love masks all that doesn't bode unwell,
It coruscates even in a darker dungeon,
Its powerful wings prove so unrelenting.

No hammer on the anvil reigns over,
No ammunition, no physical hazards,
No wall, no spatial restriction mars,
The hope of love, born in space.

The holiness that resides in all recesses,
A luminary haloed in spiritual mist,
A joyful droplet suspended in romance,
But planted solidly on the human ground.

A perennial fount didn't ever get run down,
The bloke was born in my dream, glowed,
In the mind's eye that disbelieved the real,
A lump of the priceless humankind roots for.

© Basudev Paul

Basudev Paul (Malbazar, West Bengal, India)

basudevpaul01@gmail.com

He is a poet, writer and author. His poetry is a psalm; a sacred song of his life felt at the gloaming of his career. His poetical composition aiming at the worship of God chants as a canticle for humanity. He has published one English poetry book; "The Permanent Transient". He is M.A. in English, and has worked as a teacher with thirty-seven years of teaching experience.

4. I Found My Rhythm

Wow---
I have found my rhythm...

I have escaped from the dungeon,
I hold in my hand pure sunlight,
From the sky, I pluck the stars,
I bring the moon to earth,
My feet have found their hold.

How light they have become,
They have shattered the iron chain,
Now, my steps dance,
Dance to my own heart,
No more they dance to your tunes.

I don't regret,
I raise my step,
A step for the sky,
I can't aim to break the glass ceiling,
But want to break new ground.

© Bharati Nayak

Bharati Nayak (Bhubaneswar, Odisha, India)

bharati1962@rediffmail.com

She is a bilingual poet, writer, translator and editor. She has so far published two Odia poetry collections, one book of translation of South African poetess Adiela Akkoo's book 'Lost in A Quatrain' into Odia, two English poetry collections as sole author and six books as co-author with other poets. She is a postgraduate in Political Science.

5. Unbounded Goddess

When I watch an unbounded Goddess,
To my mother feeling the divine bliss,
Whose pollen affection attended me always,
Since infancy, I do regard her caring ways.

My father bravely believed in her beautiful company,
Where the quiet peaceful life became so funny,
Keeping with the neighbours a sweet relation,
Hoisting my mother's honour like the bright glow-sun.

To make us studious and scholar ruled in one eye,
Rescuing from serious danger another eye informed goodbye.
From dawn to the deep night,
Gave labour and brain spreading minimum might.

Our dwelling house has been heaven for my mother's efforts,
Gave lessons for the singing, dancing and painting court.
To be the best travel guide took responsibility,
For her boon been so soon like great and gentle reality.

© Bidhan Chandra Roy

Bidhan Chandra Roy (Kolkata, West Bengal, India)

bidhanchandraroy24@gmail.com

He is a trilingual International writer who writes in English, Bengali, and Hindi languages. He has got many books of poems, essays, stories, novels, articles, Holy Geeta, Holy Manasamongal great epic and songs. Besides this, he is a lyricist, music composer, singer and a social worker who always prays for the world's peace. He is an M.A. degree holder, a retired Govt. officer, and a pensioner.

6. My Life

It is difficult to live,
In society nobody,
Listens to my pains,
I should make happier to all,
The family,
No one cares.
As well as listens to my problems.

I should do work at home,
As well as in the office,
I should bear children and care for them,
I should be a good daughter, wife, and mother,
Our life spends,
In many duties,
As well as responsibilities.

© Binod Dawadi

Binod Dawadi (Kathmandu, Nepal)

vinoddawadi9@gmail.com

He is a poet, writer and author. He has authored one book; 'The Power of Words'. He has worked on more than 1000 anthologies and renowned magazines. His vision is to change society through knowledge, so he wants to provide enlightenment to people through his writing skills. He is a Master's degree holder in Major English.

7. A Woman Speaks

Born with twinkling stars of emotions and dreams,
I nurse a vast sky in my eyes,
I guard my starry nights full of dreams,
Taking much care of each and every desire,
Without hurting any bee that flirts with lovely flowers.

Like soft falling showers, I kiss innocent souls,
Babies, babes, bros, sis,
And all lovable relatives,
Pouring with purity love, love, and only love,
I am the never-ending fountain of life's spring.

Yes, I am a woman, the second earth for mankind,
A possessor of unlimited patience,
A sufferer of unlimited pain,
A volcano that erupts to maintain Nature's nature,
The indomitable spirit that any age needs to have,
To create a visionary mission for future generations.

© Bipul Chandra Kalita

Bipul Chandra Kalita (Nagaon, Assam, India)

bipulkalita074@gmail.com

He is a trilingual poet who writes in Assamese, Hindi and English language. He has authored three books. He has edited many journals and literary anthologies. His writings have been published in many National and International magazines, newspapers and anthologies. He has authored nearly 26 Assamese plays. He is M.A. in English, working as a post-graduate teacher.

8. Dream of Swapnali

Her name is Mallika or may be Sewali,
Stepping on bloody petals,
With her rosy feet,
She carries dream of the forthcoming days.

She carries her tiny dreams,
In eyelids every day,
These dreams are sold,, but the price…
Puzzles sweet dreams.

She has no freedom to dream, secretly it is told,
She has no right to refuse,
If she does so, horrible results strike,
And she becomes quiet.

Her Invictus inwit allows her to win,
Who knows to taste venom, while the dream sprouts,
God even doesn't dare to shatter,
Such indomitable dreams.

© Boby Borah

Boby Borah (Tinsukia, Assam, India)

bobyborah30@gmail.com

She is a poet and author. She has authored three books and edited several magazines. Her poems and articles are published in several newspapers in Assam. She has been awarded several awards in her professional and literary journey. She is M.A. in literature, Founder/Principal of Shankardev Shishu Niketan school. She is also the president of Doom Dooma Mahila Samiti and secretary of Sundoram Kobi Sanmilan.

9. Angel

Light dances on my creamy cheeks,
An eye-kissing light,
Heart-warming light,
My elegance kindle the lamp of desires,
In the hearts of youthful minds.

I am an angel sent by God,
I spread mirth all around,
My tender affection attracts all,
The radiance of love encloses,
My very soul in all its beauty.

The enchanting charm and delight,
My offer can't be described in words,
My heart offers serenity and tranquil,
Yet, I am clueless as to why men fight,
In the name of the woman who is so divine.

© B. S. Saroja

B. S. Saroja (Bangalore, Karnataka, India)

bssaroja1953@gmail.com

She is a poet, writer and author. Her poems and writes have been published in many anthologies, magazines, and periodicals. Poetry is her lifelong passion. She is also a social worker. She is a postgraduate in Kannada and a graduate in Science and a Diploma holder in Commerce and is retired as a personal secretary to the Managing Director of a business organization.

10. Women's Empowerment

Being a woman is a blessing for the earth,
For whom the earth can get mirth,
Amongst joy, the inhabitants also get peace,
From the eternal goddess without cease.

A woman can be a mother, a sister or a daughter,
Whatever she is but she should never be a plotter,
As a woman, she should be righteous,
For she gives birth, hence should not be so desirous.

We, women, still have some desires and dreams,
So we have been fighting to fulfill in the extreme,
Many foes come and go,
But they never can bewilder us and throw.

Many storms, many floods arrive,
But we are determined to survive,
We do that not for ourselves,
But for keeping alive the human race and for themselves.

© Debashrita Basu

Debashrita Basu (Kolkata, West Bengal, India)

debashritaroy14@gmail.com

She is a passionate lover of nature. She loves to travel and her hobby is writing poems through exploring things around her and by widening her observations. She is a member of various poetry groups on Facebook. She has won several awards in literature. She is an M.A. degree holder and an English teacher by profession.

11. The Woman in You

Sometimes life never gives you a second chance,
In tough times life gave you a hundred reasons to cry,
It tested your patience, your strength indeed,
But you chose to smile instead.

Whether being a mother or wife,
The grass is always green where it is watered,
Make sure to get the best out of it,
While working on yours.

This version of you didn't build overnight,
It is the by-product of life,
Over the years you've lived,
You are not only a woman but God's wonderful gift.

© Diptirekha Das

Diptirekha Das (Bhubaneswar, Odisha, India)

diptirekhadas73@gmail.com

She is a bilingual poet and also a blogger. She has a strong passion for literature. She has contributed to many National & International anthologies. Her articles related to women's empowerment have been published in several social forums. She is a post-graduate in Economics.

12. Wo-man

A female man appearing real,
Full of beatific scents,
To work fine salvation in a dispirited man,
Long lost like an almanac out of date,
In saving wonders of sound muliebrity.

Beautiful, brave, and bold,
Long-standing like glorified sages,
En routing fine wisdom for the earth,
A near presence is all joy to the man next door,
Making healing flow freely through.

A charming human,
Ever decked In glorified beauty.

© Fagbeyide Kehinde

Fagbeyide Kehinde (Ondo, Nigeria)

owolabifagbeyide@gmail.com

He is a writer, poet, a podcaster, video editor and a chef. He is an active member of various poetry groups on Facebook. His many poems and writes have been placed in different anthologies, magazines and newspapers. He is a student pursuing Microbiology.

13. Indian Woman

They knit, cook, carry,
Weave, water, wash,
Pattern, plaster, parsimony,
Attract, dance, dictate.

Ride, drive, dog paddle,
Pigeonhole to roles,
Within and without,
And adore to be.

Battling, winning, felicitating,
Ambitious yet noble,
Honeypot yet lonely,
Conservative and ultramodern.

Penitent yet challenging,
That makes her an Indian Woman,
Pampered, pestered, fettered,
And left on an island to befriend 'Man'.

© Gargi Saha

Gargi Saha (Varanasi, Uttar Pradesh, India)

gargi.paik@gmail.com

She is a creative writer since her childhood. She has published two poetry books namely 'The Muse in My Salad Days' and 'Letters to Him'. Recently she received the Rabindranath Tagore Memorial Award and the Independence day award for poetry. She is a member of various poetry groups on Facebook. She is M.A and M.Phil. in English. Presently she edits several scientific research papers.

14. Ode to Femininity

No book, dictionary nor,
Tome of a thesaurus defines,
The very literal or metaphorical essence,
Of womanliness, a true definition of "femininity".

Whether maternal or innocent, naive or mature,
Blessed as you are with such a charming profile,
In no way do you ever deceive in "borrowed robes",
You've just enough dalliance with the 'Haut-couture" style.

Seductive, but by no means slutty,
Your attraction seems subliminal...yes, it must be said...
You certainly turn heads, and convert male legs,
Into predictable chauvinistic putty.

My ode has but scratched the surface,
Of how you might be defined as "true femininity"...
I'm sure so much more might have been included,
Due to the constraints of my poem's equanimity.

© Geoff Stockton

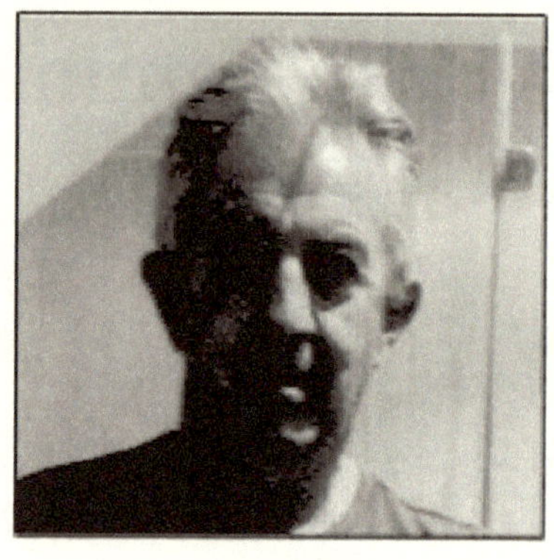

Geoff Stockton (UK)

geoff.stockton@yahoo.co.uk

He is a poet, writer and author. He has got versatile subject matter and styles of poetry and writing to pictures and themes. He also enjoys collaborative writing with other poets and mentoring the more inexperienced. He is an active member of various Facebook groups. He is B. Ed (Hons) and Cert Ed from St. Paul's College, Cheltenham, and Bristol University. He is a former English teacher.

15. I Exist

I exist....
In the coffee froth of love,
Bitter-sweet wakefulness,
And a thirst called life.

Masked memories,
Salt and peppered with time,
Hustling with today,
A savored concoction.

Womanhood is a wondrous potion,
Encompassing a universe of emotions,
A balance of strife with smiles,
Or perhaps an evolved revolution.

A multihued mix of moments that define,
Nurture Nature's nuanced dynamics,
In this heavily brewed headiness,
Let me exist as its fragrant aroma.

© Ipsita Ganguli

Ipsita Ganguli (Kolkata, West Bengal, India)

ipsitaganguli@gmail.com

She is a business consultant at sunrise and poet, travel writer and heritage, and art enthusiast at sunset. Her poems have been published in several e-magazines and anthologies. She is also one of the main characters of the poetry film Kolkata Cocktail. She has also conducted a series of online Talk Shows entitled 'Cafe Conversations' as well as curated offline Poetry events for Kolkata Literary Meet. She is a recipient of many literary Awards. She has two independent compilations of poems.

16. The Lady of Winter

The Lady of Winter, treading softly,
Invisible footsteps, dancing lightly,
Seasons turning, changing monochrome scenery,
Jack Frost weeping copiously, icicles forming.

Snow-diamonds jewels sparkle, glittering light,
Demi-parure: necklace, earrings, rime-ice delight,
Iridescent gown of verglas lacy snowflakes,
Plaid stalactite cloak - encrusted protection.

Ermine whispers, softened mistletoe slippers,
Gauntlet gloves of frosted hellebore petals,
Ice coronet tinkling, wind-chime in motion,
Bracelets of hoar-frost, charming stalagmite slivers.

Penetrating eyes, hard permafrost spheroids,
Brisk Northern winds whistle, hair - silvery curls,
Beauteous Winter walks in silence and splendour,
Woman – The Lady of Winter … My Snow Queen.

*© **Janet Stoyel***

Janet Stoyel MBE (Taunton, Somerset, UK)

j.stoyel@btinternet.com

She writes poems as her passion. She is an active member of various poetry groups on Facebook and has won several awards in poetic contests. She is a Master of Philosophy, UCE Batchelor of Arts (Hons); a Winston Churchill Fellow; Queen Elizabeth Scholar, Wingate Scholar, and Holder of: the AILU Lifetime Award. She was presented with an MBE from Queen Elizabeth II, for services to Photonics, Textiles, Art and Design.

17. Unread Story

In a way mother's mother's daughter,
A long line in one heart.

Getting up and falling,
Raise the glory in the unread story.

And unseen pain in any refrain,
But okay our server of my soul.

I know my dignity to the whole,
Being the caretaker of the breath.

Rebirth and rebirth rebuilding sacrifice,
And the woman in me is wise.

© Jurgen Uiterdijk

Jurgen Uiterdijk (Teheran, Iran)

jurgenu@icloud.com

He is a poet, writer and painter. He writes songteksts too. He is a lover of spirituality. Creativity is his aim and passion. He is an active member of various poetry groups on Facebook. He has won several awards in literature. His writings are published in various magazines, anthologies and newspapers. He is a Masters in arts and working as an Art teacher and Art Therapist.

18. Breath

To be wrapped up, with pale and long love,
Make in the newest generation, as pattern,
To tone by touch shape, recollected above,
Soul in female saved deity, day-night-span.

Aha! Find full growth, decade after decade,
In the systole and diastole to swell as film,
Ever, all settling entities still last gasp fade,
The great forms of the virtue's self to helm.

Move throu' the master the earthly manner,
Can be realized, more eternal taste silently,
To avoid, each airy as wavy thoughts clear,
Finish, enclosed era's real rescue's journey.

Love's plaited body softy as a pleasing wave,
To hide millions of truths with your tonal stave.

*© **Krishnasankar Acharjee***

Krishnasankar Acharjee (Kolkata, West Bengal, India)

krishnasankar.acharjee1122@gmail.com

He is an International freelance writer, poet and author with several Global Awards such as the Gold Pen, Gold Medal, Benjamin Award and the King of the Letters from Cuba-America. He is an English teacher and selected two honorable Doctorates from National University in the USA and Commonwealth Vocational University in the UK.

19. Salt of Life

The woman is special,
Like he fragrance of flowers,
Exuding multiple flavours.

She is light of sun rays,
Lighting the life,
A beauty of moonlight,
Spreading silver light.

An oasis in the desert,
Quenching the thirst of the soul,
Like bounteous mother earth,
Ready to grenries life.

A tabernacle in the bivouac of life,
Giving shade and shelter in her heart,
Real Goddess of love incarnate,
Showering her with affection and care.
Earth intolerance with generous heart,
And above all, SHE IS SALT of Life.

© Krishna Walikar

Krishna Walikar

(Gokak, Karnataka, India)
krishnawalikar55@gmail.com

He began his literary Journey eight years back and his main hobby is literature and music. He wrote many poems in Kannada and English. He won several awards in poetry. He is President, Admin, moderator and Group expert in International poetry groups. He is B.A. and a retired Administrative Officer of the Education department of the Government of Karnataka.

20. Benevolence of Woman

The real beauty of a woman is her pious nature,
Sacrifice and tolerance featured in her life's character,
Love and sacrifice are reflected in her behavior,
Nurtures the existence with her pious signature.

Spontaneous loving service reflected by her compassionate zeal,
Protect the life of kith and kins by natural will,
Faith, hope, and charity are the ornaments of a woman,
Manifests every existential prosperity of the nation.

Environment goes to uphill momentum of her words and deeds,
Uphold the dharmic attributes with concentric moods,
Adjust the growth of life by concentric administration,
Exalting far-sighted intelligence in possible conditions.

Every step of women do better for society,
Worship and welfare are the passion for positivity,
Love and compassion are materialized with simplicity,
Special distinctiveness makes life solidarity.

© Dr. Laxmikanta Dash

Dr. Laxmikanta Dash (Sukinda, Odisha, India)

drlaxmikantadash1967@gmail.com

He is a multi-faceted personality who has excelled in his proficiency in various fields of art and culture. As a bilingual poet, his many poems have been translated into Indian and foreign languages. He is an active member of various poetry groups on Facebook. He is M.A, M. ED, PH. D, D. LITT in Education. Presently, he is serving as HOD, of Education at Sukinda College, Odisha, India. He has garnered numerous accolades from India and abroad.

21. A Woman's Strength

When a woman falls in love,
She's so compassionate,
With undeniable passion,
Gives love without commission.

She journeyed the slippery path of her life,
Stumbled but stand, pursuing to reach the top,
No turning back or have a stop,
Her undiminishing strength gave her pride.

A woman shines like the stars in the sky,
For she perseveres since from the start,
To achieve her goals, be successful in life,
Like most men did she also did her part.

The woman is to be honoured and praised,
With her achievements that she had raised,
For a woman can do a manly task,
Competitively done, not to mistrust.

© Lilia Luis

Lilia Luis (Lamitan, Phillippines)

hellosydney1215@gmail.com

She is a poet, artist, singer, dancer and a majorettes trainer. She is an active member of several poetry groups on Facebook and keeps on contributing her writings there. She is a retired teacher with 32 years of service. She earned her Bachelor's Degree in Education (BSEED) and Master of Arts in Education, majoring in Administration and Supervision.

22. For All Times

Women are wonderful,
Women are great,
Women are special.

A paradise for the eyes,
The soul seeks peace,
Because they are special.

They gave it to me,
Strength every day.
I spread love,
To all women again,
Because I am great.

When I share love with women,
Women are miracles of God,
But I know they are warriors,
When you get angry just once,
For all times...

© *Maid Corbic*

Maid Corbic (Bosnia and Herzegovina)
detrix233@gmail.com

He is a young writer who is passionate about poetry. He also selflessly helps others around him. He is the moderator of the World Literature Forum 'World Literature Forum Peace and Humanity' in Bhutan. He is also the editor of the First Virtual Art portalled by Dijana Uherek Stevanovic and the selector of the competition on a page of the same name that aims to bring together all poets around the world his face. He is a diploma holder in graphics and web design.

23. I Love Myself

Soft, serene, sensuous, soulful,
I have a glowing face, physic wonderful,
Everyone turns back, looks at me parsimoniously,
I feel proud but pretend to look shy.

I love myself, my well-undulated body,
Dressed as a sophisticated, elegant lady,
The woman is considered a replica of beauty,
Few emotional worship as Divine Deity.

For centuries, she was used to please the mighty kings,
She had lived a long, very long night of distress,
Each and every woman had a painful story,
But why I'm being sympathetic to the bygone.

She has squeezed space for herself, with no mercy,
Let's take it as inspiration to grow and shine,
So that, nobody dares to touch, harm,
Because I'm a woman.......

©Manjula Asthana Mahanti

Manjula Asthana Mahanti

(Bhubaneswar, Odisha, India)
manju.a.mahanti@gmail.com

She is a trilingual poet, author, editor, translator and storyteller. She has got eight collections of books and her writings are a part of National, and International anthologies, e-magazines, etc. She is the recipient of several awards from Gujarat and Telangana Sahitya Academy along with the "Icons of Asia " Award recently. She is a postgraduate in Sociology and Hindi, Graduatte in English, Honors, Sangeet Prabhakar (vocal), and B. Ed. She worked in college as Senior Lecturer, and last as a high school Principal.

24. Like Water

Like colorless water, I flow in your realm,
Merge with everyone, with multiple names like a river or stream.
Gurgles and roars always carry a fresh surge,
And I do not flow in reverse.

I may look vulnerable, but I am not feeble,
I move forward, gushing through rocks and pebbles.
I have an indomitable spirit, I am a woman,
Why is gender bias between women and men?

Capable like men, bright like the rays of dawn,
In my womb, life leaps like a fawn.
Few tried to destroy me.
And endeavors to stop my flow and contaminated me.

Still, no one can stop my dynamic motion
Like an effervescence river, I flow towards my primordial ocean.
As I have fathomless patience, I can make my way,
Like a bird and wind, I fly and sway.

©Mousumee Baruah

Mousumee Baruah (Gurgaon, Haryana, India)

mousumimamu@rediffmail.com

She is a bi-lingual freelance writer and poet. Many of her poems and short stories are published in various National & International literary platforms, anthologies, blogzines, etc. She has won several awards in her literary journey. She is the author of the poetry collection, "The Castaway". She is a Master's in English. She worked as a Lecturer.

25. You Don't Know Me

You have seen me crying,
All teary-eyed and broken,
For someone might have gone,
Leaving me all alone.

You have seen me withering,
Like an unwatered plant,
In the absence of love,
Craving like the Eve.

You have seen me melting,
From love, duty, sacrifice, pity,
With my vulnerabilities,
Etched on the corners of my lips.

You have seen all the times,
that magnified my weaknesses,
But you haven't seen me,
For you just know the surface.

© Nosheen Irfan

Nosheen Irfan (Lahore, Punjab, Pakistan)

noshy.qureshi194@gmail.com

She is a poet by heart. She has contributed to various international poetry anthologies on topics of great relevance to the current times. She holds a Master's degree in English Literature and is a teacher by profession.

26. Sister's Love

O' my dear sister,
Your love is as clear as water,
Your word strikes as iron,
You indeed shine as a diamond,
You are a wonderful treasure.

You stood and I stand,
Your world bless me,
Your love flow as a river,
I do pray to be your twin,
Aha! we will do everything together.

© Okechukwu Chidoluo Vitus

Okechukwu Chidoluo Vitus

(Onitsha, Anambra, Nigeria)
jlcmedias@gmail.com

He is a poet, coach, author, evangelist, blogger and publisher. He has won several awards in vivid poetry competitions. He is the manager at JLC Media. He has written five books. He is an active member of various poetry groups on Facebook. He holds the degree of Master's in Education.

27. She Is a Woman

She's a woman..
A soft touch of the morning breeze,
A sensual touch of the sunbeam,
The warm embrace of the clouds,
And a vivid beauty, full of grace.

She's a woman..
An elixir of your soul spirit,
The taste of rain in a barren land,
A fragrance of petrichor on parched earth,
A soothing melody solacing the heart.

She's a woman..
Wears a smile even in pain,
Bleeds inside to give a birth,
Though fragile, she's your strength,
Holds you firmly to make you strong,

A creator, warrior, and fighter she is!

© *Pragyan Parimita Nanda*

Pragyan Parimita Nanda (Guwahati, Assam, India)

m123.nanda@gmail.com

She is a trilingual creative writer in Odia, Hindi, and English languages. She writes in different journals both Print and magazines, plus on online platforms Instagram and Facebook. She is a homemaker, a trained journalist, a voracious reader and a passionate writer who loves to travel and explore new places. She is M. A in Journalism.

28. She Never Told

She never told her love in words,
But linked us together when broken,
Flew to and from morn till evening star, in the sweet smile,
Like berries of our garden.

We lived in clusters swaying in wind,
As little grass on her lap of Lea,
The guide of our untraveled world,
The teacher in her never I found in schools.

How often I remember her voice, the whisper is but an illusion,
Plucking flowers in our garden,
How death is a word for alive I understand,
Feel unsure of her response though I call.

There is nothing so worthy when we learn her own shattering,
The spring turning into a winter landscape,
I knew she wouldn't stay long here,
Contained in us an end from the beginning.

© Rajender K Padhi

Rajendra K Padhi (Bhubaneswar, Odisha, India)

rajendrapadhi62@gmail.com

He is a poet, novelist, editor and translator. He has translated many stories, biographies and poems from Odia into English. He has written 5 books including poetry and novels. His articles, poems and interviews are published in more than 80 books, and journals from different countries of the world. He has been a keynote speaker address in both National and International conferences. He is retired as a Professor in English.

29. When She Is in Severe Need

The woman is God's gift to this universe,
She is a symbol of great sacrifice,
She is a treasure to human beings,
She does so many beautiful things.

A woman is God's most beautiful creation,
God's biggest and greatest expression,
He gifted her with beauty and great courage,
In tough times men just have to encourage.

He also gifted her a monthly companion,
It's neither a disease nor contagious,
It is God's other gift to a woman,
Which makes her more courageous.

Periods are nothing but biological cycles,
Don't make difficulties for her survival,
Know the facts, learn the actual reality,
Let us give her all the much-needed serenity.

© Rajesh Sharma Brahmabhatla

Rajesh Sharma Brahmabhatla

(Khammam, Telangana, India)

rajeshpa09@gmail.com

He is a bilingual poet. He writes in English and Telugu languages. He is an Admin of various poetry groups on Facebook. He has authored one English poetry book entitled 'Hey Honey'. His writings are part of several anthologies, newspapers and magazines. He has received many awards for his poetry. He is BSc in Computer Science and presently works for the Government of his state in the Panchaytraj Dept.

30. Life Moves On

All alone my life moves on,
Not at all, I am unhappy or lonely,
The morning sun lits up my lawn,
With its radiance.

I forget the meaning of sadness,
I smile and focus on my job, workplace,
Where at times the scorching sun blaze,
And I amunable to gaze,

On the day that brings light and hope as a blessing,
Then I close my eyes and sing,
The song of glory to the divine mother,
Under her care, I consider myself a philosopher.

Who moves on with her self-styled philosophy,
To perceive joy and happiness as a trophy,
From the heavens,
Where receive the handful of grains.

*© **Rimni Chakravarty***

Rimni Chakravarty (Siliguri, West Bengal, India)

rimnichakravarty@gmail.com

She is passionate about poetry, music, art and literature. She has got more than 50 publications, 6 book chapters, and two best paper presentation awards in quest of reaching a platform in the world of literature. She is M.A.(English), B.ED, Asst. Professor and Humanities.

31. My Odyssey Continues

In circumstances adverse, I stand tall,
Like the queen of plants to you, I call,
Learn to bloom out of crevices and gaps,
Be master of your own fate, adorn your caps.

Fine, frail, fragile, and flamboyant I am,
But strong is my will to rise and stand,
Circumstances to thrive are hard to find,
But with my grit and determination, I will rise.

From a fledgling, I will grow with roots stout,
Tempests and windstorms cannot sign me out,
Ye all! I Strive to thrive, applaud my efforts,
Soft in disposition, small in size I overcome all hazards.

In the game of survival, I am bound to emerge victorious,
Slowly but steadily I traverse the path with insightful ingenious,
Nobody can terminate my dreams as I rise high,
My odyssey continues till I attain my sky.

© Ritu Kamra Kumar

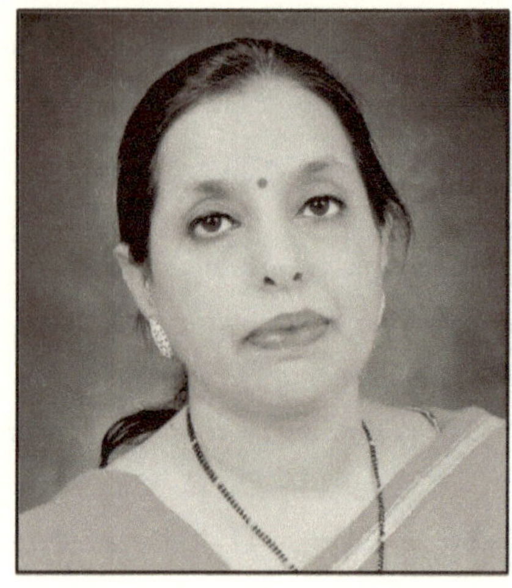

Dr Ritu Kamra Kumar (Yamunanagar, Haryana, India)

ritukumar.gmn@gmail.com

She is an avid writer, poet and academic. She has contributed more than 350 write-ups, articles and poems in several National newspapers and magazines, and many research papers in National and International research journals and anthologies. She is the Editor in Chief of her College magazine. She has authored three books. She is M., M. Phil, and Ph.D. in English literature, and working as a HOD and Associate Professor in the Post graduate Department of English.

32. She Too Was a Woman

She too was a woman
Who was none other
But my mother....

Who has now become
A twinkling star
In the sky so far
Who made me sleep
With her sweet lullaby
And taught me
"Twinkle twinkle little star
How I wonder what you are"

Now really I wonder about her
No more I could hear her sweet lullaby
My voice too does not reach to her
She has gone so far
Which song can bring back her?

© Rohit Dash

Rohit Dash (Bargarah, Odisha, India)

rohitdash28@gmail.com

He is a multilingual poet and writer. He writes in Odia, English, Hindi and Sambalpuri languages. So far 24 of his books has been published. He is a member of various poetry groups on Facebook. His works are also published in many International anthologies and E-zines. He has received many awards and recognition for his poetry. He is M.A. in English and is retired as a Bank Manager.

33. You're Amazing One

In this vast canvas of earth,
So many mysterious arts,
Among all of those,
You're amazing dear.

As a woman,
You can say boldly,
Not a single touch of fear,
You will nourish golden love.

You know yourself better,
You can do anything on earth,
You try to make glorious art,
You have passed so many exams.

Salute my dear friend,
As a gem on earth,
The world is so proud,
To get you here as a divine part.

© S Afrose

S Afrose (Dhaka, Bangladesh)

afrosewritings@outlook.com

She has been writing since 2020. Poetry is her best friend. She has published two books- "Thanks Dear God" and " Poetic Essence". She is a member of various poetry groups on Facebook. She is B Pharm, M Pharm from Jahangirnagar University.

34. My Mother - A Strong Woman

My mother - a strong woman,
A woman of grit,
Fiercely independent,
Till she passed away at eighty-six.
A woman who faced all situations,
From the front,
She never used the words 'I can't'
She never thought anything was beyond her,
And as her daughter,
That is what I learned from her.

I am a woman and from my mother, I learned,
The sky is the limit,
I worked hard at everything I did,
I achieved things I never thought I could,
I excelled as an educationist,
I became a writer and a poet,
Something that I had never imagined.

© Sabita Pillay

Sabita Pillay (Trivandrum, Kerala, India)

sabita@pillays.net

She is a poet, author and writer. Poetry is her passion. She has published two solo books. She is an active member of various poetry groups on Facebook. She is M.A, BED. She has worked in the field of education for more than thirty years in India, Singapore, and Hong Kong. Back in India now.

35. Uncovered

Breathing through the covers came,
A mild tug, searching for my modesty,
To break it free from the shackles of morality.

My feet were then turning ripples.
Along a forest path,
Witnessing the breaking of a silent night,
Hooting like black birds that shout their hearts out,
On the spire of your castle.

The tug kept drawing my feet to eternity.
Searching down my beads of sweat,
Moulding into dews on the forest floor.

While they met the lightning, raging black clouds,
Baying for blood, for her modesty,
That she hid so well, behind her gilded cage.
You just had to touch it,
You just had to break her free.

© Saheli Mitra

Saheli Mitra (Kolkata, West Bengal, India)

moonchitu15@gmail.com

She is a social entrepreneur, journalist, author and poet, who runs her own content and creative company, 'Tales Talks & Walks' with an experience of 25 years as a journalist. She has got more than 200 published articles to her credit. She is an author of the Internationally launched romantic thriller 'Lost Words' and a co-author of several short story collections and poetry anthologies. She is M. Phil in Environmental Biology.

36. Daughters

Angelic souls on the earth,
Generous and loving at heart,
Flourishing physiques overall,
They are labelled as 'daughters'.

Tenderness in their actions,
Soothing voices in speech,
Connecting human beings,
They are adorably called 'daughters'.

Leaving your sweet home a day,
They create another loving home,
Chivalrous outside, sensitive within,
They're embraced as 'daughters'.

Mentally stronger than men,
Eternal skillul challengers,
Quick opportunity grabbers,
They prove they're capable 'daughters'.

© Setaluri Padmavathi

Setaluri Padmavathi (Hyderabad, Telangana, India)

sreenipad@gmail.com

She is a creative artist, bilingual poet and writer. Her stories, articles and poetry have been published in reputed magazines and e-journals. She is a Postgraduate in English literature with B.Ed., She has been in the field of education for more than three decades.

37. Heaven on Earth

Crystal drops of dew on the fresh green leaves,
A whisper of divine love by the morning breeze,
Carrying the dust of the heavens beneath her feet,
Mother is the version of God being discreet.

Holds a baby in her womb, than ever in the heart,
Nothing except death could make them apart,
In heaven also wait for each other to meet,
Mother is the version of God being discreet.

An epitome of selflessness and sincerity,
Among all her children there's no disparity,
The birth of a child makes her feel complete,
Mother is the version of God being discreet.

The melody of her soothing voice creates harmony,
The mere touch of a sacred hand ends the agony,
Her love saves the children from the searing heat,
Mother is the version of God being discreet.

© Shafia Afzal

Shafia Afzal (Islamabad, Punjab, Pakistan)

afzalshafia5@gmail.com

She is a bilingual writer and poet. She writes in English and Urdu. Reading and writing have been her passion since childhood. She's a member of several renowned literary forums on social media. Her articles have been published in various National newspapers. She holds a degree of B.SC, in Statistics, Mathematics, and Economics.

38. Me and Myself

Let me introduce myself,
I am born alike,
Welcome me too,
I will survive and surprise.

Fittest of the survival,
I have survived and I will,
I have climbed Mount Everest
I will cope up too with the necessary evils.

I am a keen observer,
I am a keen believer,
I am worshipped as Shakti,
When needed, I deliver.

I have seen contradictions,
I have withstood the outlook and practices,
Empowerment is in laws and regulations,
The struggle is continuing in my endeavours.

© Shelleyandra Kapil

Shelleyandra Kapil (Chandigarh, India)

kapilirts@gmail.com

He is a poet, reviewer and writer, who writes in Hindi, Punjabi and English languages. He has published 6 books. His poems are published in various literary magazines, books, newspapers and anthologies. He has achieved several awards in his professional as well as literary fields. He is M.A in Public Administration. He has retired as Principal Chief Commercial Manager from North Central railways, Prayagraj.

39. Radha

Because I am a woman...
They never care to blame,
Your dulcet or its magic notes,
That inveigled me out of,
My unsullied world to you,
Passionate arbour, but always stick to,
My soul the label of a coquette,
Brand me a transgressor, and shove me,
Down to a vortex of infamy,
And look at me.

It is I, the woman of disrepute,
The symbol of profanity,
Stand redeemed in love,
Beside you, your holy queen,
In the holy shrines set up by,
The keepers of the holy law.

© Dr. Snehaprava Das

Dr. Snehaprava Das (Bhubaneswar, Odisha, India)

dassnehaprava@gmail.com

She is an eminent poet and translator. She has translated several Odia fictions, nonfictions, plays, and poems into English. She has five collections of English. She has received the Prabashi Bhasha Sahitya Samman, the Fakirmohan Anubad Samman and the Jibanananda Das award for her translations. She is M.A, and Ph. D in English.

40. Versatile

I am a woman, a poet and a doctor,
An artist, a singer and an embroiderer,
An ordinary chef and an interior decorator,
Introverted by nature and a silent observer.

Lead a low-key life with very few friends,
Don't follow fashion blindly, and set my own trend,
My family is the place where my heart stays,
Especially my kids, around whom my life sways.

Among all my roles, being a doctor is the most difficult one,
As it brings a sense of responsibility and reason,
All other roles can take second place to accomplish,
But when it's about the patient's life, then you need to rush.

Sometimes, by God's grace, I cure the patient,
But at times, I explain to them about palliative intent,
Then I counsel them to trust the one, who is omnipotent,
With a faith that God will bless them, with happiness and health.

© Dr. Suboohi Jafar

Dr. Suboohi Jafar(Varanasi, UP, India)

suboohijafar@gmail.com

She is a young and dynamic poet, artist and singer by heart, an oncologist by profession. A Soldier in Fight against CANCER. She has won many awards and medals in her academic career. She has received several awards in poetry contests conducted by various poetic groups on Facebook.

41. Woman Is Like a Glider

Eve, the first woman of God's creations,
Her sin, opened the doors for redemptions.
Frailty thy name is woman !, by writer GBS,
But all have sinned and living by grace.

A woman is like a glider,
Independent is she: makes herself a leader.
Not inferior to man in every fields, today,
Examples are many as the hope of ray.

Often a single woman is a successful mother,
Difficulties give her strength, never to bother.
Woman is like earth, bears everything,
Composer of songs, and she can also sing.

Accepting defeat is not in her dictionary,
Goes on fighting till the end, with making merry.
She is a woman, but not at all weak,
Strong enough to conquer the Himalayan peak.

© *Sudhir Kumar Nanda*

Sudhir Kumar Nanda (Calicut, Kerala, India)

sknanda205@gmail.com

He is a bilingual poet, writer and author. He writes articles, short stories and quotes. He has published a poetry book entitled 'psalms of Life' and a novel entitled 'Fatal adolescence'. He has achieved several awards in literary contests. He is an active member of various poetry groups on Facebook. He holds a master's degree in Economics and Psychology, and Diploma in Creative Writing in English.

42. Paragon of Power

O' my Goddess, Durga, you are the absolute power.
I beg you to offer me an indomitable spirit.
I seek the courage to thwart my cowardly nature.
Thou are the paragon of beauty like an ever-glowing light.

I pray you, Ma, everywhere there is chaos,
Our life is like a nightmare,
In this pandemonium, I am utterly voiceless,
A foetus is disfigured by the demons.

Lusty creatures are chasing the women,
With your divine manifestation, let you alter the disasters,
As a paragon of glory, you endow me with vigour,
I crave to suppress evil powers.

With thine blessings, I will tread on,
This will be a miracle for this lost civilization,
Let the unseen powers rewrite,
History with an altered vision.

© **Sudipta Mishra**

Sudipta Mishra (Bhubaneshwar, Odisha, India)

sudiptamishra71@gmail.com

She is a multi-faceted artist and dancer excelling in various fields of art and culture. She has weaved more than a hundred books. Her book, 'The Essence of Life', is credited with Amazon bestseller, and 'The Songs of My Heart' is scaling newer heights of glory. She has garnered numerous accolades in literature, including the famous Rabindranath Tagore Memorial. She regularly pens articles in newspapers as a strong female voice. She is a research scholar, perusing a Ph.D. in English.

43. Sympathy

I can stand criticism, curse, or mockery,
but sympathy makes me feel like a street dog.

People say I am happy with a secured job,
a stuffed wallet and a carefree life,
but I know the number of wakeful nights,
I have spent shedding silent tears.

Let the people be ignorant of,
the truth and let my calculated pretence,
provide me some sincere comforts.

I am afraid of raising my glittering robe of laughter,
lest somebody would see my heart bleeding.

I don't want to aggravate my pain,
with deceptive words of consolation from selfish persons,
Alone it is much easier to face suffering.

© Sulekha Samantaray

Sulekha Samantaray (Bhubaneshwar, Odisha, India)

sulekhasamantaray54@gmail.com

She is a bilingual writer with twelve published books and hundreds of articles including stories, poems, essays and translations both in English and Odia languages. She has also received many literary awards for her contribution to literature. She is M.A and M. Phil in English and retired as an Associate Professor in English.

44. The Crystal Lady

The multifaceted artistry of the divine,
World! A barren land without woman.
Bloomed like a rose from man,
Bold and beautiful, a multitasker.

Commendable in grooming society,
Ingrained within, the creator and destroyer
An epitome of sacrifice and love,
Torchbearer of culture and tradition.

Nurturing like a mother,
Juxtaposed with work and life.
Tossed about by hurdles,
Resilience her trait.

Takes pride in motherhood,
Incredibly powerful and fierce.
Yet gentle and pure,
A crystal to be handled with care.

© Sulochana Narayanan

Sulochana Narayanan (Palakkad, Kerala, India)

sulsubra@gmail.com

She is a lover of arts like paintings, music and poetry. She has recently published her first book "Imprints: An Anthology of Poems". She is a member of various poetry groups on Facebook and has won several awards. She is M.A English and has done B.Ed. She is an academician by profession for the past 11 years.

45. Bond of Birth

I'm a woman, the bond of birth.
The union of every relationship on the earth,
The evergreen fragrance of nature,
And the ethics of every immortal page.

When waves were created in the stream,
When stories were written between the river and sea,
When the trees put on the green leaf,
I'm the bond of birth with the pure ethics of love.

When beauty was created in the universe,
When serenity kissed the hills or valleys,
When echoes of the heart were heard in the peak mountain,
I'm the bond of birth with relics of scarification.

Between the earth and azure sky,
Between the soil and water,
Between the air and fragrance,
I'm the bond of births, the temple of motherly love.

© Sumi Kapahera

Sumi Kapahera (Morigaon, Assam, India)

debend557@gmail.com

She is a poet by passion. At present, she is involved with many wonderful poetry platforms and literary organizations. She has achieved many awards including Gujarat Sahitya Academy certificates. She is an M.A. in English and BED, a teacher by profession.

46. Woman of Destiny

Dancing demurely in divine design,
A woman of destiny, a marvel so fine,
No one can deny her purpose divine,
She is a beauty of a different kind.

Gleaming gracefully, her gaze meets the sky,
A vision of victory, and a winner high,
None competes with her power and might,
A symbol of strength and a marvelous sight.

Courageously she follows her own way,
A determined diva and a leader today,
No one can deny her infinite worth,
She is a goddess of greatness on earth.

Majestically she moves with such ease,
A warrior of wisdom, a spirit of peace,
No one can quench her fire and zeal,
She is a queen in the greatest story to tell.

© Tshewang Norbu

Tshewang Norbu (Tashi Yangtse, Bhutan)

tnorbu90@gmail.com

Born into a family of readers, he is very much fascinated by poetry and short stories. He has also received several awards and appreciation for his poems and essays as well. He is a member of a few writer's groups and participates in contributing articles frequently. He holds a Post Graduate Diploma in Public Administration.

47. A Second Grade

Considering me, a commodity and a second-grade citizen,
Addressing the weaker sex, quoting the entire phenomenon,

The essence of my existence gets crushed and buried in the dungeon,
My identity gets shrunken to a worm pinpointing as a woman.

Dying untimely death, facing the partiality of the world inhuman,
Each step gets faltered and stability altered in this motion.,

I am not defeated, I raise with vigorously rigorous notions,
Slaining all the beliefs of this taboo of underprivileged inhibitions.

Creeping out from the shell of the cocoon witnessing the light of the moon,
I obtain my status, with my fervent perseverance of devotion,

The t ime comes sooner, to realize the power of the woman,
Gradually she becomes a pivot behind the success of the men.

The journey is tough from time immemorial society's patriarchal is of
men,
An era of fresh fate is engraving, the world of women.

© **Uma Natarajan**

Uma Natarajan (Ratlam, MP, India)

uma1948@yahoo.com

She is an artist who uses words as her medium, She has published 15 books of poetry in English and 2 books of Hindi poetry. She has contributed various articles in various books in English and Hindi. Her dream is to continue writing and contributing to the field of literature. She holds Masters in English.

48. Bhima and the Flower

That day an enchanting breeze brought fragrance unknown,
Draupadi's irresistible passion soared deep inward.
Her loving husband was at her beck and call to service, ever,
And he with his heavy club was on his way to gather.

Weary paths, woods, and all never hindered his march,
It was a determined march never to be forsaken now,
But an old monkey that lay was a terrible obstacle for him,
To please a wife was godly, ever craved by the chivalrous.

Such unexpected events, ill-omen of course occurred,
And his club was used to move the tail in the path,
The mighty one, ready to please his lady attempted again,
Lo! His muscles were at a tearing point, and the tail was still.

Shivering, looking aghast, lost his ego, the mighty one,
What would his dear one think about this fiasco terrible,
Until his brother incognito revealed himself and blessed,
Such are stories that the epics celebrated in India.

© Unnikrishnan Atiyodi

Unnikrishnan Atiyodi (Kannur, Kerala, India)

uatiyodi@gmail.com

He is a poet and writer with 3 collections of poems in English and also essays in English entitled 'Spectrum'. He has written three books in Malayalam and contributes regularly to e-journals. He is the winner of Sahithyamanjari Puraskaram. He has also received the best teacher award.

49. Who is She?

A marvel,
A miracle,
Filled with mystic potions.

An enigma,
A riddle,
Full of countless solutions.

A panacea,
An elixir,
Overflowing with myriad emotions.

A saga,
A parable,
Inscribed with extraordinary caution.

She is the basal,
The cardinal,
Exuding the essence of our existence.
She is…a woman.

© Vandana Oke

Vandana Oke (Delhi, India)

vandanaoke111@gmail.com

She is a poet, writer and author. She writes stories, articles and poems. She is actively spilling her ink on various social media groups, winning accolades and rising on her own writing graph every day. She is thoroughly enjoying her plumage in this deep ocean of the literary world. She is an Arts graduate from Delhi University. She worked as a Pre-primary teacher for many years.

50. A Woman's Load

A woman's load is always heavy,

But she smilingly carries,

Her burden of responsibilities,

She can never say no,

And is always ready to do more.

With love in her heart, she walks on,

However difficult the way,

However hot the day,

Winter or summer, she works hard,

And gives her best to her family.

She tries to keep everyone happy,

She works inside the house,

And manages her career too,

And balances on the tight rope,

With her heart strong and true.

© Vasudha Pansare

Vasudha Pansare (Bangalore, Karnataka, India)

vasudhapansare@gmail.com

She is a poet, writer and author. She has contributed to several anthologies. She has also won several literary awards. Her hobbies are reading, writing, reviewing, traveling, music and films. She has published four volumes of poetry. She is a gold medallist in English literature with BA and MA and is retired as HOD in English.

www.ingramcontent.com/pod-product-compliance
Lightning Source LLC
Chambersburg PA
CBHW022013150726
47990CB00002B/642